THE STATE OF FOOD INSECURITY IN JOHANNESBURG

MICHAEL RUDOLPH, FLORIAN KROLL,
SHAUN RUYSENAAR & TEBOGO DLAMINI

SERIES EDITOR:
JONATHAN CRUSH

Cover Photograph: Florian Kroll

© *AFSUN 2012*

ISBN 978-1-920409-76-0

First published 2012

Production by Bronwen Müller, Cape Town

AUTHORS

Michael Rudolph is the Director: Siyakhana Initiative for Ecological Health and Food Security.

Florian Kroll is the Programme Head: Siyakhana Initiative for Ecological Health and Food Security.

Shaun Ruysenaar was an MA student at Wits University and is now in the PhD programme at the University of Edinburgh.

Tebego Dlamini was formerly a researcher at Wits University.

Previous Publications in the AFSUN Series

No 1 *The Invisible Crisis: Urban Food Security in Southern Africa*

No 2 *The State of Urban Food Insecurity in Southern Africa*

No 3 *Pathways to Insecurity: Food Supply and Access in Southern African Cities*

No 4 *Urban Food Production and Household Food Security in Southern African Cities*

No 5 *The HIV and Urban Food Security Nexus*

No 6 *Urban Food Insecurity and the Advent of Food Banking in Southern Africa*

No 7 *Rapid Urbanization and the Nutrition Transition in Southern Africa*

No 8 *Climate Change and Urban Food Security*

No 9 *Migration, Development and Food Security*

No 10 *Gender and Urban Food Insecurity*

No 11 *The State of Urban Food Insecurity in Cape Town*

ACKNOWLEDGEMENTS

We would like to acknowledge the staff of the Johannesburg Directorate of Social Assistance for contributing field researchers, Sabelo Dlamini for co-ordinating the field researchers, and Edmore Marinda for doing additional statistical analysis. The editor and authors would like to thank CIDA for its financial support of the African Food Security Urban Network (AFSUN) through the UPCD Tier One program.

CONTENTS

FIGURES

TABLES

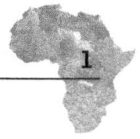

1. INTRODUCTION

Johannesburg is the economic hub of South Africa and the Southern African region as a whole.[1] The city is located in Gauteng Province, the industrial and commercial heartland of South Africa. Gauteng is the source of 33% of South Africa's Gross Domestic Product (GDP) and 50% of all employee remuneration in the country.[2] Only three African countries have larger economies than this single South African province. The Gauteng city region is expected to grow to 14 million inhabitants by 2015, putting it in the top 15 urban areas in the world by population.[3] The region comprises three metropolitan areas: Johannesburg, Ekurhuleni and Tshwane. Johannesburg is the 40th largest urban agglomeration in the world and has been described as one of only two "Global Cities" in Africa.[4] The metro area provides 16% of South Africa's GDP and is home to 40% of its economic activity.[5] Johannesburg's Human Development Index score is around 0.7 which puts it amongst the highest in South Africa. Between 1996 and 2001 the population of the city grew at 4.1% p.a.[6] In 2007, Johannesburg was home to at least 3.9 million people, and the metropolitan area as a whole was estimated to have a population of over 7 million.[7]

Aggregate measures of Johannesburg's demographic and economic growth and prosperity mask complex underlying socio-economic inequalities and cultural tensions.[8] Unequal access to land, housing and basic services is a fundamental legacy of Johannesburg's history. Current settlement and land tenure patterns, as well as grossly inadequate housing, were shaped by the implementation of policies of racial segregation.[9] The apartheid legacy, urban poverty, rising unemployment and an inability to provide adequate services to the rapidly-growing urban population exemplify the "hidden structures of marginality and social insecurity" challenging city managers and residents.[10]

The 2008 Johannesburg Poverty and Livelihoods Study noted that "the urban poor, residing in certain pockets of the city such as informal settlements and inner city areas, are particularly vulnerable and struggle to gain access to services and opportunities to improve their livelihoods."[11] Although the post-apartheid national and local governments have attempted to address this situation, widespread inequality persists. As one recent study notes: "New housing developments have largely taken place on the outer edges of existing townships, far away from jobs, facilities and services. This has marginalised new settlements and contributed to the further fragmentation of the urban fabric of Johannesburg. State-subsidised housing .... often means dislocation from job opportunities and

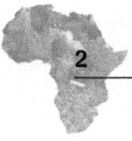

social services. The greater transport costs of accessing these amenities have increased the net financial burdens placed on state subsidised house-holders who may have previously occupied better-located sites in slums or informal settlements."[12]

Johannesburg has a massive backlog of services from the unequal and inefficient systems of municipal government bequeathed by the apartheid state.[13] Rapid urbanisation puts additional strain on already over-stretched basic services and city infrastructure. The scale of demographic growth and urbanisation in South Africa suggests that Johannesburg's develop-ment challenges will only intensify in the coming years. These entrenched patterns of spatial and economic inequality, dislocation and marginalisa-tion impact on peoples' ability to participate in the urban economy and thus on their ability to access food. At the time of the last Census in 2001, half of Johannesburg's households earned below the national minimum of R1, 600 per month.[14] Disparities in wealth are further reflected in exten-sive food insecurity throughout the city region.[15] Urban food security is an emerging concern and fundamentally different to challenges of food insecurity in rural areas and the agricultural sector.[16]

Little is known about the extent of food insecurity in Southern African cities, making it difficult for development practitioners and policy makers to quantify the challenge and to pro-actively plan to reduce the urban food gap. In order to address this gap, the African Food Security Urban Network (AFSUN) undertook a baseline urban household food security survey in 11 SADC cities in 2008-9. The University of Witwatersrand's School of Public Health (a member of AFSUN) undertook the survey in Johannesburg. The survey focused on trying to understand the prevalence of food insecurity and its relationship to poverty in the poorer areas of the city. Three contrasting sites were chosen in different parts of the city: Orange Farm, Alexandra and the inner-city area of Joubert Park. The three areas all have many poor and food insecure households but they also have different geographies, histories and socio-economic and demo-graphic profiles. The AFSUN survey therefore afforded an important opportunity to examine how poor households in different geographical localities within a large urban conurbation experience and respond to food insecurity. The study, and this report, do not purport to address the food security situation in Johannesburg as a whole but do provide insights into the situation in three "typical" poorer areas of the city.

FIGURE 1: City of Johannesburg

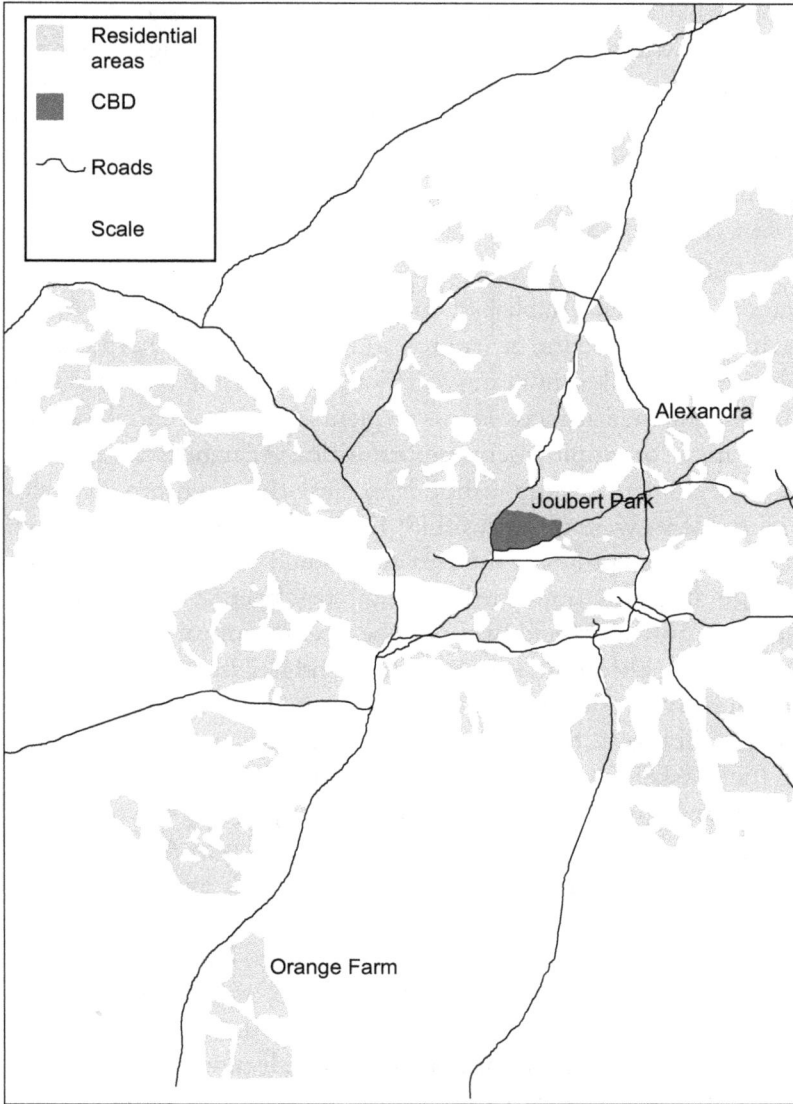

2. METHODOLOGY

Three distinct areas of Johannesburg were chosen for this study of food insecurity in the city (Figure 1):

- Joubert Park is a high-density residential Inner City area which had a population of 40,000 in 11,537 households at the time of the 2001 Census. At the Inner City Summit in Braamfontein on 5 May 2007, the Mayor of Johannesburg, Amos Masondo stated optimistically that: "The inner city is the symbolic, economic and cultural heart of

Johannesburg and is strategically important to the city as a whole." He noted that the revitalisation of the inner city "was a catalyst for economic growth and job creation, as well as for creating a work and living environment that was secure and decent."[17] Currently, however, thousands of people living in the inner city of Johannesburg are poor, unemployed and go to bed hungry. Women, children, the elderly and people living with HIV (PLHIV) are the most vulnerable.[18] Ward 60 and some households from Wards 63 and 64 were included in the survey (Figure 2).

- Alexandra is a well-established formal township area close to the up-market business centre of Sandton and the affluent northern suburbs of Johannesburg. Alexandra was founded as a township for Africans in 1913, and remained attractive to its residents due to its central location and proximity to employment opportunities. Apartheid-era pressure from more affluent neighbourhoods to clear the township and relocate its residents were unsuccessful.[19] Despite overcrowding and poor services, and perceptions of the area as a hotbed of crime and hostility to foreign migrants, rapid urbanisation has been a key feature of Alexandra's post-apartheid history. The massive influx of job-seekers from rural areas throughout South Africa and neighbouring countries put an already overloaded infrastructure under increasing pressure. Living conditions in the congested informal settlements, hostels and along the Jukskei river are unhealthy and stressful.[20] The area is a mix of formal and informal housing but has thriving markets and good access to transport networks. The total population of Alexandra was estimated at approximately 350,000 in 2002, with estimates varying between 180,000 and 750, 000. San Kopano precinct (Ward 75) and East Bank (Ward 105) were selected for the study. East Bank is a more recent expansion of Alexandra, with more formalised housing and clearly demarcated properties. The San Kopano precinct is part of the older historical core of Alexandra, and is much more congested and informal. In 2001, the Ward 75 population was 42,000 living in 9,482 households. Around 25% of adults were unemployed.[21]

- Orange Farm is on the southern fringes of Johannesburg and is characterised by extensive low-cost informal housing. The settlement was founded in 1988 and is now home to an estimated one million people. The unemployment rate is close to 50%. Orange Farm is considered the largest informal settlement in the country with most residents living in shacks. Despite construction of formal low-cost RDP houses and the provision of pit latrines to stands not connected to sewer systems, Orange Farm has experienced regular service delivery protests focused on the lack of proper houses, sewerage services, running water and electricity. The 2001 census indicated that only

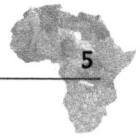

35% of the Orange Farm population was employed, far lower than the national average of 45%. According to one study, over 23% of the population in Extension Two was HIV positive in 2008.[22] Wards 1, 2, 3 and 4 were selected for the survey. They had a population of around 26,000 and 5,802 households in 2001. The area is the poorest of the three study sites and Ward 3 is one of the poorer wards in Orange Farm.

FIGURE 2: AFSUN Survey Sites

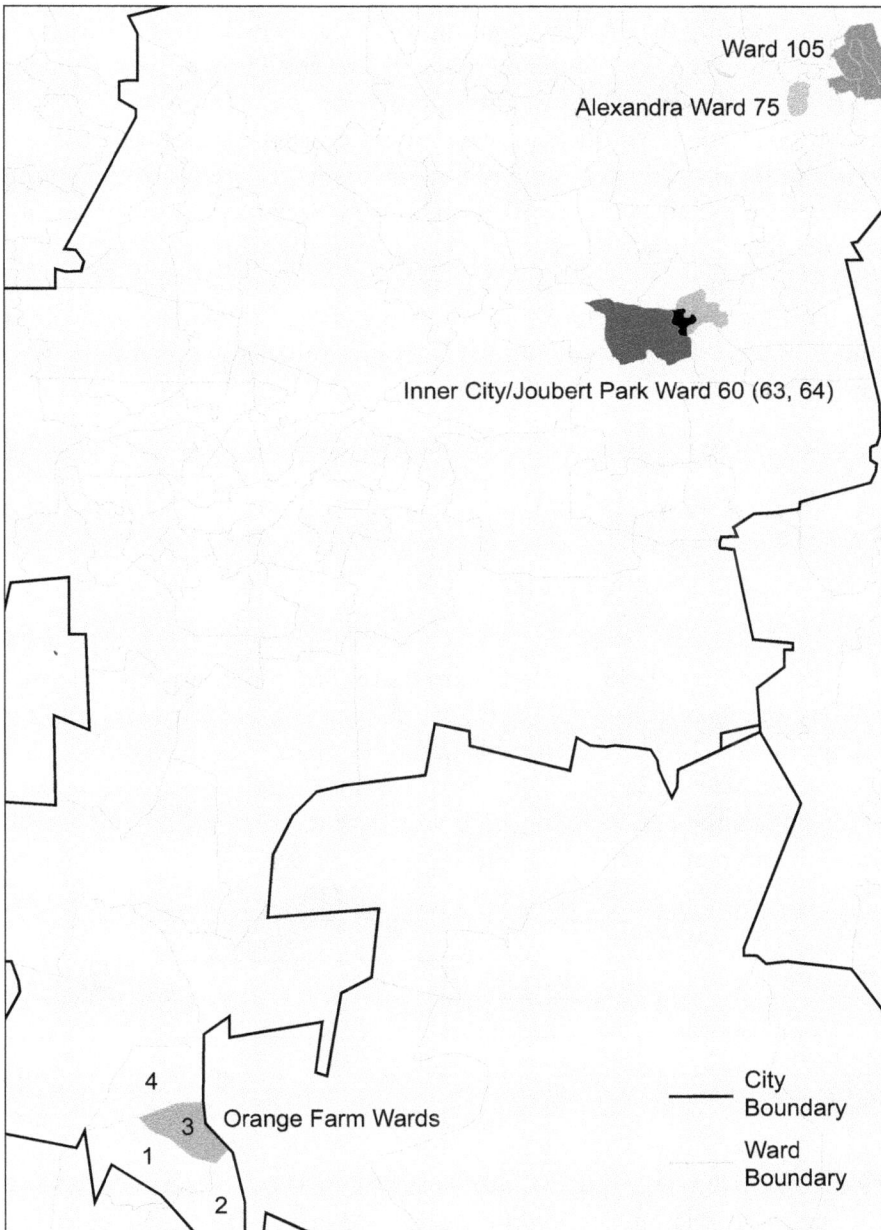

Ward 105

Alexandra Ward 75

Inner City/Joubert Park Ward 60 (63, 64)

4

3 Orange Farm Wards

1

2

City Boundary

Ward Boundary

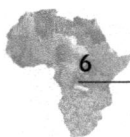

A total of 996 households (comprising 3,762 individuals) were sampled in the three sites. A systematic sampling method was chosen but given the limited time frame, transport and the small team, spreading the researchers throughout the research clusters was impractical. Every tenth household was interviewed rather than every 30th predicted by the initial sampling equations.

The research instrument used in the survey was developed by the AFSUN partners at a workshop in Botswana in 2008 and implemented in all 11 SADC cities surveyed.[23] The collection of the data was organised and implemented by the Health Promotion Unit at Wits University in partnership with the City of Johannesburg (Social and Human Development Unit). One element of this partnership was the involvement of Community Development Youth who were mobilised and invited to participate in a training workshop as potential fieldworkers. Fifteen of these young adults were joined by fieldworkers who were recruited by an inner city organisation with which the HPU had previously worked. A total of 32 people participated in the initial training workshop but only 16 of the participants undertook the fieldwork. Most of the fieldworkers had experience in research or were exposed to community projects so they were capable of carrying out the survey.

3. SOCIO–DEMOGRAPHIC PROFILE OF THE SAMPLE

The average household size in all three sites combined was 3.8. Household size ranged from 1 to 12. Eighty six percent had between 1 and 5 members, and 14% of households had more than 5 members (Table 1). Household sizes differed slightly in the various study areas, with households in Orange Farm tending to be somewhat larger (with 18% having more than 5 members).

TABLE 1: Household Size			
No. of Members	Alexandra %	Orange Farm %	Inner City %
1–5	89	81	88
6–10	11	18	12
>10	0	1	0

Households can be grouped into seven main types, based on the sex and primary relationship of the household head: (a) female-centered or headed households (usually single women, widows and separated/ divorced/abandoned) without a spouse or partner; (b) male–centred or headed households without a spouse or partner; (c) nuclear households of immediate blood relatives (usually male-headed but spouse or partner present); (d) extended households of immediate and distant relatives and non–relatives (again usually male-headed with a spouse or partner also present); (e) female-centred juvenile households (under 18 years of age); (f) male-centred juvenile households (under 18 years of age); and (g) "other" households which fit none of these categories.

Over one third (37%) of the total sample were nuclear and another 15% were extended households (Table 2). A further 14% were male-centred, meaning that 66% of the households in total had a male head. Slightly less than one–third of the households (29%) had a female household head. Some noteworthy differences emerged between the different study areas. Orange Farm, for example, has the highest proportion of female-headed households (at 35%) and the Inner City the lowest (25%). Orange Farm also had a much smaller proportion of male-centred households (9% versus 15% in Alexandra and 18% in the Inner City). The proportion of juvenile-headed households was very low all three areas. However, such households are comparatively rare throughout South Africa, a reflection of strong social and kin networks who take in children orphaned by HIV and AIDS.[24]

TABLE 2: Household Structure				
	Orange Farm %	Alexandra %	Inner City %	Total %
Female-centered	35	28	25	29
Male-centered	9	15	18	14
Nuclear	38	41	33	37
Extended	16	15	16	15
Juvenile-headed (female)	0	0	1	1
Juvenile-headed (male)	0	0	1	0
Other	2	0	6	3

The age profile of household heads also varied across the city (Table 3). In all three areas, the majority of household heads were between 30 and 50. The older established area of Alexandra had a significant number of older household heads (29% over 50 and 13% over 60 years of age). However, the newer area of Orange Farm actually had more elderly household heads (38% over 50 and 20% over 60 years of age). This may be because many of Orange Farm's residents moved there from other areas in the city (such as Soweto) because the cost of housing was much lower.[25] The Inner City, with its much more fluid migrant population, had the youngest household

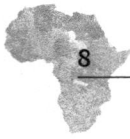

head profile (with 46% of heads under the age of 40 compared with 34% in Orange Farm and 40% in Alexandra).

TABLE 3: Age Profile of Household Heads				
	Orange Farm %	Alexandra %	Inner City %	Total %
>20	1	0	1	1
20-29	11	16	22	16
30-39	23	24	38	29
40-49	26	30	25	20
50-59	18	16	9	15
60+	20	13	7	14
N	341	292	332	965

The general youthful profile of all household members in the three sites was apparent (Table 4). As many as 62% of the whole sample was under the age of 30 and nearly 40% were under 20. On the other hand, the proportion of elderly residents was comparatively low. Only 10% were over 50 years of age and 4% were over 60. What this means, at a general level, is that social grants in the form of pensions are unlikely to be a significant contributor to the income of many households. On the other hand, child grants are likely to be of some importance. Orange Farm had the highest proportion of children (42%) and the Inner-City the lowest (35%). The Inner City had the highest proportion of working-age adults and the lowest proportion of the elderly.

TABLE 4: Age Profile of Household Members				
Age Group	Orange Farm %	Alexandra %	Inner City %	Total %
0-10	17	16	16	16
10-19	25	22	19	22
20-29	19	23	28	23
30-39	15	15	19	16
40-49	11	13	12	12
50-59	6	6	4	5
60+	7	5	2	4
N	1,411	1,043	1,163	3,617

Finally, with respect to the educational profile of the sample, half had a high school education but only 16% had gone on to obtain a tertiary qualification (Table 5). Alexandra and the Inner City had many more residents with a tertiary education than did Orange Farm. As many as

13% of the population had no formal schooling. However, this includes the 8% of the population who were between the ages of 0 and 4. What this suggests is that the earning potential of households in Orange Farm is potentially lower than that in the other two areas. This is compounded by the fact that these areas are close to potential formal sector employment opportunities, whereas Orange Farm is geographically more remote.

TABLE 5: Level of Education				
	Orange Farm %	Alexandra %	Inner City %	Total %
No formal schooling	13.3	11.6	12.8	12.6
Primary school	23.8	19.5	18.5	20.8
High school	52.5	46.1	51.9	50.5
Tertiary education	10.4	22.8	16.8	16
N	1,411	1,043	1,163	3,617

4. LEVELS OF HOUSEHOLD FOOD INSECURITY

Levels of food security in Johannesburg are principally related to household income and the ability to access food through purchase. Four measures were used in the study to capture the various dimensions of food insecurity. The first measure is the Household Food Insecurity Access Scale (HFIAS) developed by Food and Nutrition Technical Assistance Project (FANTA).[26] The HFIAS score is a continuous measure of the degree of food insecurity in the household in the previous month. An HFIAS score is calculated for each household based on answers to nine 'frequency-of-occurrence' questions. The higher the score, the more food insecurity the household experienced. In the analysis, the households were then grouped into four categories (severely, moderately, mildly and not food insecure) according to their individual HFIAS score. The survey found that a total of 56% of households were food insecure with 27% severely food insecure (Table 6).

The three study areas exhibited important differences in levels of food insecurity (Table 6). Theoretically, levels of food insecurity ought to be higher in impoverished informal settlements than in the more diverse Inner City. And indeed, 34% of households in Orange Farm are severely food insecure compared with only 26% in the Inner City and 21% in

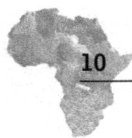

Alexandra. However, when severely and moderately food insecure households are combined, the gap between Orange Farm and the Inner City closes (47% each). There is also virtually no difference between the proportion of food secure households in each area. Alexandra shows a very different profile with 54% of households food secure and only 33% moderately or severely food insecure.

TABLE 6: Household Food Insecurity				
	Food Secure %	Mildly Food Insecure %	Moderately Food Insecure %	Severely Food Insecure %
Orange Farm	40	13	13	34
Inner City	39	14	21	26
Alexandra	54	13	12	21
Total	44	14	15	27

A 2007 University of Johannesburg (UJ) study found higher levels of food insecurity in many parts of the city, including in Orange Farm and Alexandra (Table 7). Overall, the UJ study found that 41% of households were severely food insecure, 26% were moderately food insecure and only 27% were food secure (compared with figures of 27%, 15% and 44% in this study). Marked differences between the two studies were also evident in Orange Farm (62% versus 34% severely food insecure) and Alexandra (49% versus 21%). Only the UJ areas of Riverlea and Diepsloot had similar HFIAS scores to those found in this study.

The primary reason for the different findings in the two studies is that different types of households and areas were sampled. The UJ study targeted the poorest areas of the city and all but two of the wards chosen fell into the poorest 25% of wards of the city.[27] One (in Orange Farm) is the poorest of Johannesburg's 109 wards. Our survey included areas such as East Bank (Alexandra) which include more formalised housing and a relatively higher level of affluence. Similarly, the Orange Farm sample included the poorest ward but also sampled households from three other less-deprived wards. In addition, the two studies used different sampling techniques. The UJ study drew a sample of 100 stands in each administrative area, which, due to different settlement densities, resulted in varying numbers of households sampled in each area. In Orange Farm, for example, only 112 households were surveyed, while our study (with its different sampling technique) interviewed 341 households in Orange Farm.[28] Another possible source of the difference in findings is that levels of food insecurity do vary throughout the year. Although there is no

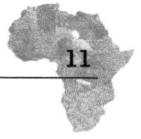

indication what time of year the UJ study was conducted, our survey was implemented in November when levels of food insecurity are generally lower than during the previous four months.

These findings are therefore not necessarily contradictory but rather illustrate different aspects of the food security experience. The UJ study provides a snapshot of food insecurity in the poorest wards of the city while this study illustrates that there is diversity across the city, and even within some of the city's more deprived areas. The findings certainly highlight the fact that food security status is very dynamic across time and space, and that great care should be taken not to generalise findings from specific areas to the city as a whole. This is especially important in Johannesburg which has such marked socio-economic differences between closely adjacent neighbourhoods.

TABLE 7: Household Food Insecurity in Johannesburg				
	Food Secure %	Severely Food Insecure %	Moderately Food Insecure %	Mildly Food Insecure %
Riverlea	48	27	20	5
Doornkop	10	51	31	8
Phiri/Senoane	25	37	26	12
Diepsloot	49	29	19	3
Alexandra	25	49	21	5
Jeppe	27	37	31	5
Orange Farm	10	62	22	6
Ivory Park	27	45	23	5
Total	16	41	26	7
Source: De Wet et al, Johannesburg Poverty and Livelihoods Study, p. 21.				

Overall, female centred and nuclear households reflected the highest levels of food security (at 46.3% and 46.4% respectively). Fewer male-centred households (42%) were food secure but this was higher than the 36% of extended families. Some 24% of nuclear households indicated severe food insecurity, followed by 25% of female-headed households, 34% of extended households and 34% of male-headed households. Contrary to expectations, female-headed households therefore appeared to be less likely to experience severe food insecurity than male-headed or extended households.

A second measure of food insecurity used in this study is derived from the Afrobarometer's Lived Poverty Index (LPI), which provides a subjective experiential index of "lived poverty." The LPI measures how often people report being unable to secure a basket of basic necessities of life including food.[29] The LPI has proven to be a reliable, self-reported, multi-dimensional measure of deprivation. Comparing the results for food sufficiency for the three study areas, the LPI shows that the Inner City actually has the highest proportion of households who say they "always" go without food (14% versus 11% in Orange Farm and 9% in Alexandra). However, Orange Farm has the highest proportion who say they always/regularly go without food (41% versus 39% in the Inner City and 32% in Alexandra).

A third measure of food insecurity attempts to capture the quality of the diet of the urban poor. FANTA's Household Dietary Diversity Scale (HDDS) was used to measure the degree of dietary diversity in Johannesburg.[30] The HDDS refers to how many of the 12 food groups were consumed within the household in the previous 24 hours. The results show reasonable dietary diversity in all three of the study areas (with HDDS scores highest on average in Alexandra (8) and lowest in Orange Farm (at 7.2). However, it is also clear that a significant minority of households in each area score below the community mean (Figure 3).

FIGURE 3: Distribution of Dietary Diversity Scores

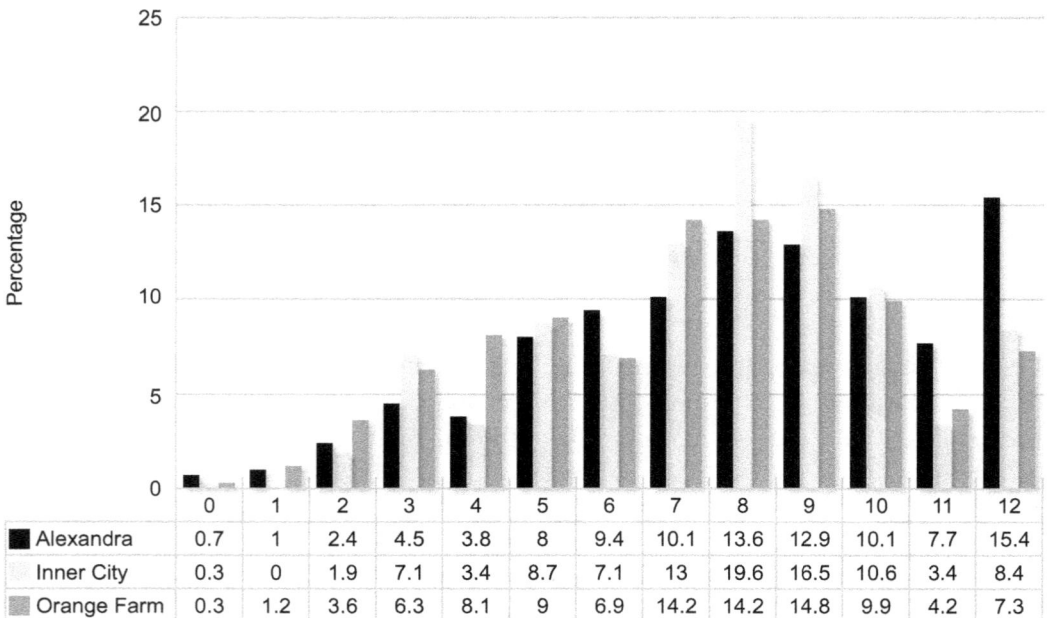

	0	1	2	3	4	5	6	7	8	9	10	11	12
Alexandra	0.7	1	2.4	4.5	3.8	8	9.4	10.1	13.6	12.9	10.1	7.7	15.4
Inner City	0.3	0	1.9	7.1	3.4	8.7	7.1	13	19.6	16.5	10.6	3.4	8.4
Orange Farm	0.3	1.2	3.6	6.3	8.1	9	6.9	14.2	14.2	14.8	9.9	4.2	7.3

In Alexandra, for example, 33% of households had a score of 6 or less and 12% had a score of 3 or less. The equivalent figures were 35% and 11% in Orange Farm and 29% and 9% in the Inner City. A Dietary

Diversity Score is regarded as low if it is below a value of 4.[31] The data shows that about a third of households in all three areas lack the kind of dietary diversity that is considered a pre-condition for good health. The survey also revealed a marked tendency for unhealthy eating. Calorie-dense, low-fibre and micronutrient-poor food groups predominated, with substantially lower consumption of fibre and micronutrient-dense pulses, fruit and vegetables, and a high prevalence of sugar and fat in the diet. These dietary patterns could be linked with the patterns of chronic illness such as diabetes, obesity, hypertension and cardiovascular disease.

The final measure of food insecurity used in this study addresses the reliability and regularity dimension of food security: FANTA's Months of Adequate Household Food Provisioning Indicator (MAHFP).[32] The MAHFP captures changes in the household's ability to ensure a regular supply of food throughout the year. Households were asked to identify in which months (during the past 12 months) they did not have access to sufficient food to meet their household needs. A significant number of households in all three areas indicated that they had experienced several months of inadequate food provisioning: 43% in Orange Farm, 34% in the Inner City and 27% in Alexandra. Orange Farm households consistently reported the highest number of months of food shortage. Overall, January, February and March were months in which the greatest numbers of households reported food shortages, with slightly elevated numbers reporting shortages again from August to November. These "slow" months are largely unrelated to the agricultural cycle since the types of foods purchased most by households are available year round. Rather, they may reflect periods of household recovery from periods of increased expenditure related to public holidays and festive seasons.

FIGURE 4: Months of Adequate Household Food Provision

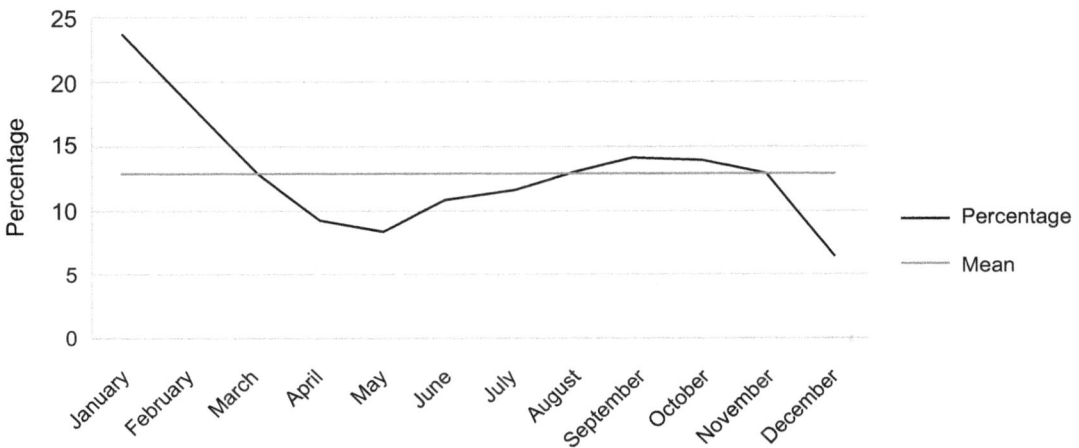

5. FOOD INSECURITY AND HOUSEHOLD INCOME

Food security in Johannesburg is linked directly to household income. Most households in the survey said they rely on a single income strategy; 60% had no additional strategies and only 26% one additional strategy. The primary income source for all households was wage work (47% of households), followed by pensions, disability grants and other allowances (19% of households), and casual work (8%). Only a very small percentage of households reported income from formal or informal businesses (around 2% each). The most important source of employment income was skilled work (21% of households), followed by office workers, managerial workers and civil servants (16%), unskilled labour (16%), professional employment (15%), businessmen/women (11%) and military/security (10%).

There was considerable variation across the city in the occupations of household heads (Figure 5). Most of the professional and clerical categories were more important in the Inner City than in the other two areas, although Alexandra had the highest proportion of skilled workers. Orange Farm had the highest proportion of job-seekers, a finding consistent with the higher rates of unemployment in that area. It also had the largest proportion of households who rely on pensions as their primary income source. Less than 3% of households overall were dependent on the informal economy as their primary income source.

FIGURE 5: Household Head's Primary Occupation

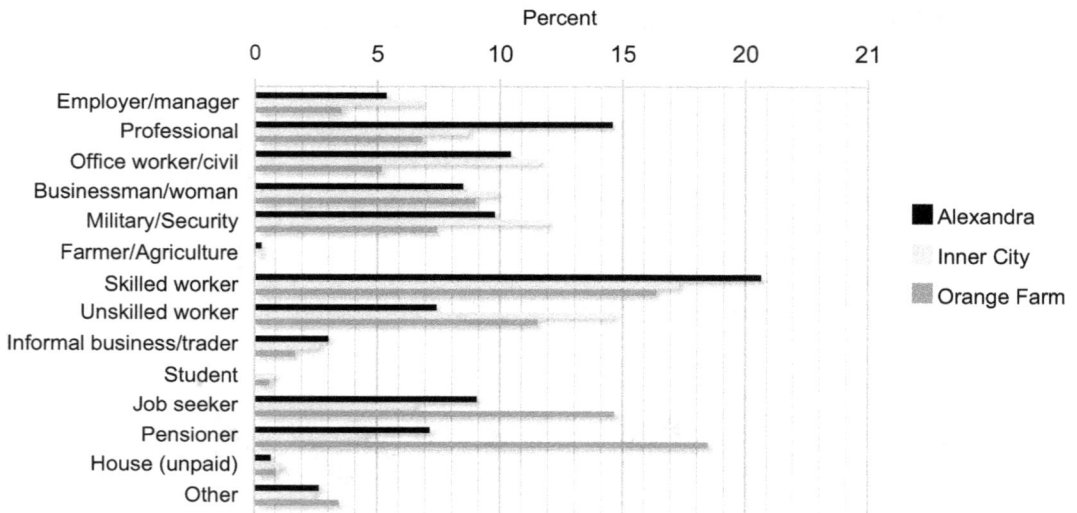

Household incomes are consistent with this general pattern of greater accessibility to and professional work in the Inner City and to skilled work in Alexandra. Incomes earned from the same occupation also vary, presumably because of differential access to better-paying work. For example, office workers and skilled workers from Alexandra earn considerably more than those from Orange Farm. Informal sector workers earn most in the Inner City, followed by Alexandra and then Orange Farm. Unskilled workers earn very similar amounts in all three areas. The net result of these spatial variations in access to employment and better-paying jobs is considerable income variation in the three areas. Average monthly household income for the surveyed households was R7,391 in Alexandra, R5,424 in the Inner City and only R3,854 in Orange Farm. About one-third of economically active respondents earn less than R2,500 per month.

There is a clear relationship between employment, income and food insecurity. Households with a full-time working member are significantly more likely to be food secure (Figure 6). Households with a member in part-time or casual employment are slightly more likely to be food secure. Households with a member who is actively looking for work are, as expected, more food insecure. The primary anomaly is the 40% of food secure households who reported that the household head was not working and not looking for work. For this to happen, the household must have other income sources (such as child grants).

FIGURE 6: Household Head Employment Status by Food Security Status

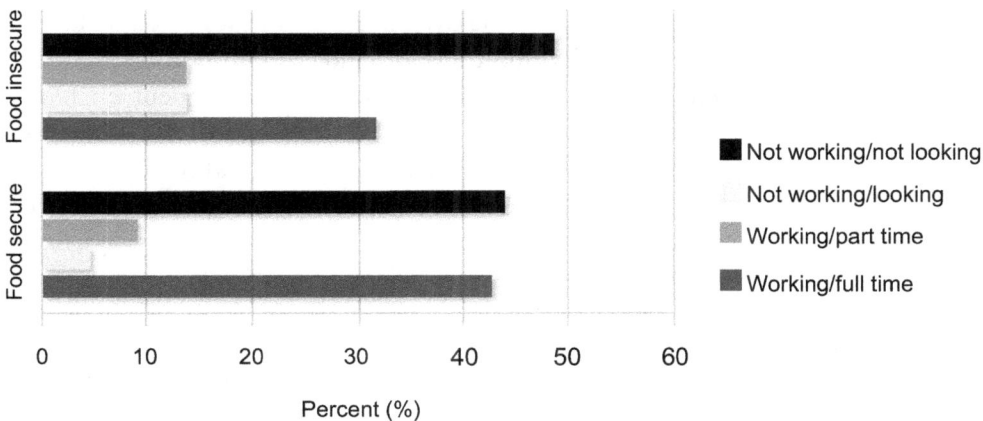

The relationship between actual income levels and food security is even clearer. The large majority of food insecure households are in the poorest income tercile and the greatest concentration of food secure households are in the upper income tercile (around 50% in each case) (Figure 7).

Some 20% of households in the upper income tercile are food insecure, a definite reflection of the fact that absolute incomes are still very low even for the 'better-off.' On the other hand, around 23% of households in the lower income tercile are food secure, presumably because these are smaller households with fewer dependants or are food secure through the judicious use of social grant income.

FIGURE 7: Household Food Security Status by Income Tercile

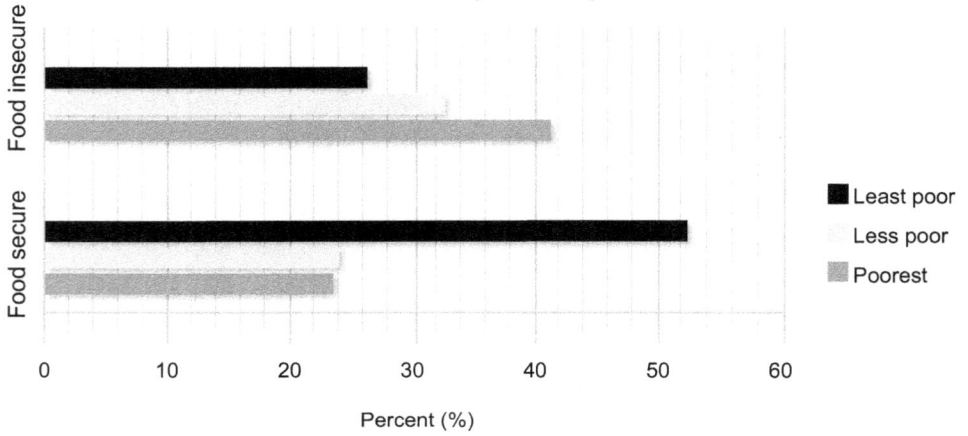

In general, the poorer the household, the greater the proportion of household income that is spent on necessities such as food. According to Statistics SA, 26% of household consumer expenditure by black African households is on housing, water, electricity, gas and other fuels, furnishings and routine maintenance of the dwelling.[33] This is followed by food, beverages and tobacco at 23% and transport and communication at 21%. The survey found that the proportion of income being spent on food easily exceeded the national average (at 35%). Expenditure was highest in Orange Farm (41%), followed by Alexandra (36%) and the Inner City (27%). The overall reliance on the cash economy and the inadequacy of alternative livelihoods and food sources is reflected in the large proportion of income which the lowest income tercile spends on food (Figure 8).

The survey was implemented during a period of major increase in the price of food. More than half of the households reported that they had had to go without food at least once a month in the previous six months because food was not affordable. More than 40% of food insecure households had gone without food more than once a week in the previous six months (Figure 9). Households in Orange Farm were most affected, with 24% reporting regular shortages of food due to price increases and 33% reporting occasional shortages.

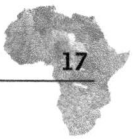

FIGURE 8: Percentage of Income Spent on Food by Income Tercile

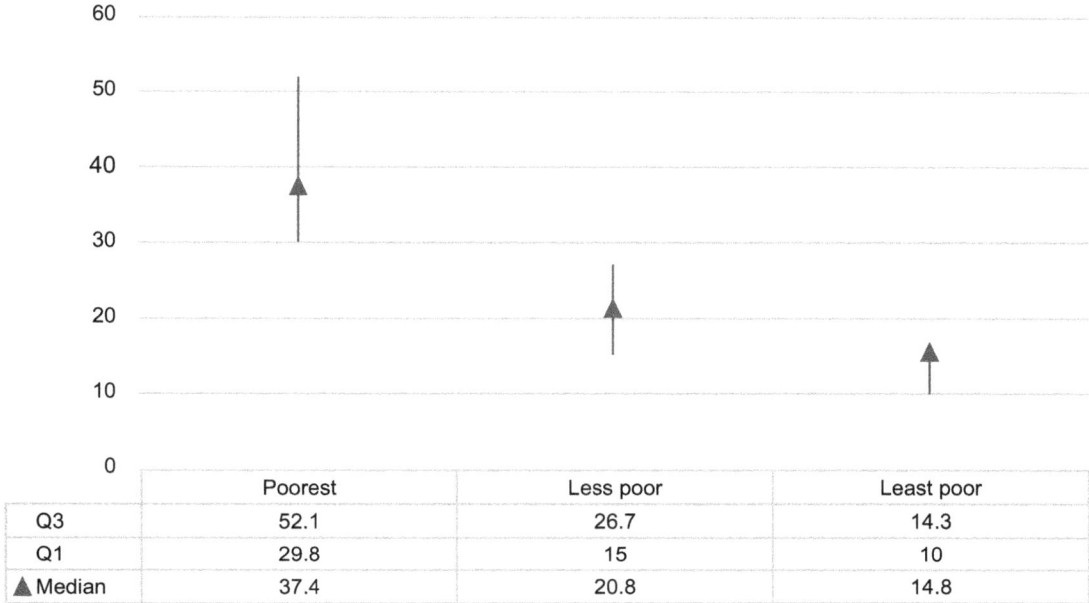

	Poorest	Less poor	Least poor
Q3	52.1	26.7	14.3
Q1	29.8	15	10
▲ Median	37.4	20.8	14.8

FIGURE 9: Households Reporting Food Shortages Due to Unaffordable Prices

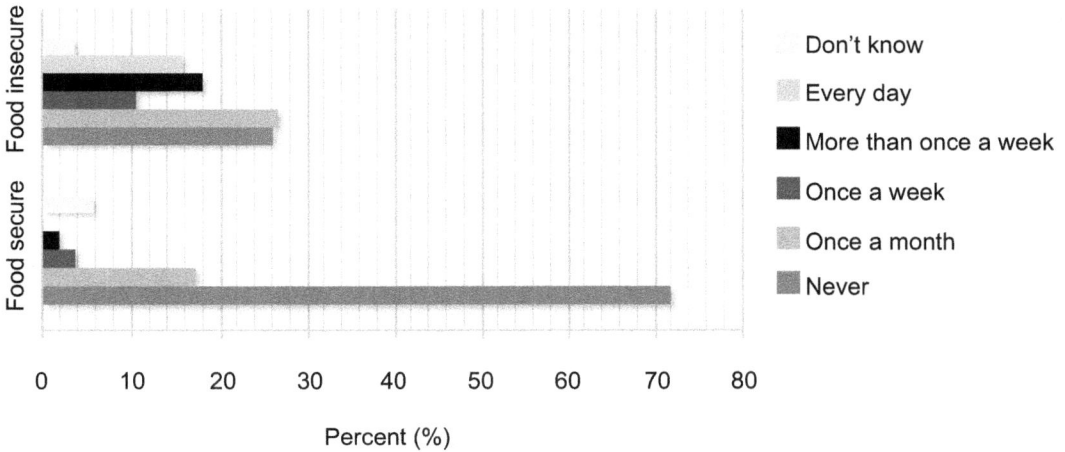

6. SOURCES OF FOOD FOR THE URBAN POOR

The vast majority of the food consumed by households in the survey was purchased. The structure of food systems, i.e. the networks of production, distribution, sale and consumption, therefore play a major role in the food security of the population. Food systems in Johannesburg are currently in a state of considerable flux. Johannesburg's poorer communities participate strongly in the informal economy of street foods and roadside vendors. However, the informal economy is probably best understood as a food security survival strategy with inadequate support from state or civil society.[34]

The informal economy is known to be a major source of food for poorer households in South African cities.[35] The survey confirmed the importance of informal food sources in Johannesburg. More than 70% of households source food from informal markets or roadside stalls at least once a week or even more often (Figure 10).

FIGURE 10: Frequency and Types of Food Source

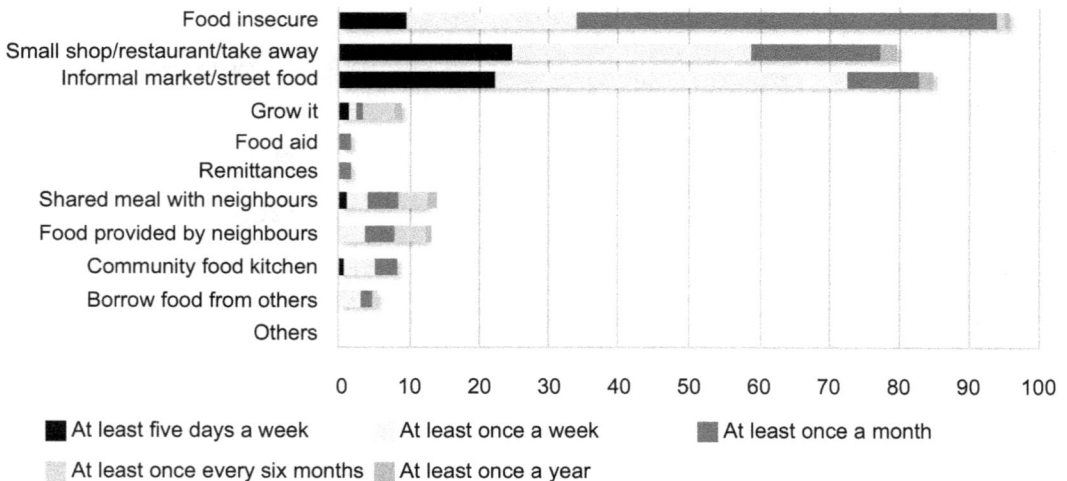

Just over 20% patronize informal sources on an almost daily basis. The preference for foods sourced from informal vendors may be linked to high levels of mobility and long-distance commuting within the city, to the difficulty and cost of transporting large volumes of food from supermarkets, and to inadequate cold storage in households which may not have fridges or electricity and the ability to pay for the electricity. Informal food

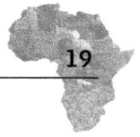

was more frequently sourced for day-to-day and weekly provisioning, although its importance for daily provisioning was greatest in the Inner City. Small shops, restaurants and fast food outlets also play an important role in day-to-day provisioning amongst the urban poor. More than 55% of households source food from these outlets at least once a week or more often. They are patronised more frequently in the Inner City and least often in Orange Farm. This may reflect the fact that the density of the Inner City makes small food enterprises more viable, supporting a greater range and number of such food access points.

The formal economy is dominated by a handful of supermarket retail chains, which are rapidly increasing their reach, even into poorer areas.[36] Supermarkets are more often associated with the urban middle-class and are seen as of little relevance to the food security of poor households:

> The burgeoning of supermarkets in developing countries may not be of immediate relevance for the urban poor. Large chains are unlikely to establish a significant presence in slums or ghettoes any time soon. Even if they appear at the periphery of poor settlements, they may not be convenient for the poorest slum dwellers if they lack transport or cash to purchase in bulk. It is also not clear that the prices offered at supermarkets would be attractive enough for the poor to make them change their purchasing patterns in the short term. Supermarkets may also have a negative effect on employment, since many of the poor work as food vendors or transporters.[37]

However, the survey found that supermarkets are actually an extremely important food source for poor urban households in the city. Over 90% of surveyed households purchase some of their food at supermarkets although Inner City respondents visit supermarkets slightly more frequently than respondents from other locations. Just over a third purchase food from supermarkets at least once a week. Supermarkets are patronized less frequently than informal sector outlets, and more likely to follow a monthly or weekly rhythm. This suggests that they are used to secure staples like maize meal, sugar, and oil in bulk, as these items are less perishable and easily stored. The less frequent use of supermarkets also reflects constraints in terms of access and transport to larger shopping centres where most are located, as well as lack of access to cold storage of perishable goods.

The FAO has noted that supermarkets are impacting on food supply chains as well as the types of food that consumers can access:

> The supermarket and shopping mall phenomenon ... attracts consumers away from the traditional small community stores and erodes traditional community life, yet can increase the range and cross-seasonal

availability of foods, albeit at a cost to local food supplies. Supermarket suppliers tend to be large producers who can provide guarantees of quality (nutritional and safety) and reliability, thus gradually eliminating smaller farmers who are less able to meet these standards or production quotas. This further undermines small-scale farming as a livelihood, and these farmers find themselves with little choice other than to migrate to the cities.[38]

One of the implications for the urban poor is greater and more regular access to staples provided that they have the income to make the purchases. The modern urban food system is also producing changes in dietary habits that accompany more urban lifestyles, including increased consumption of coffee, carbonated beverages, sugar, meat and offal and potatoes.[39] Urban dietary patterns are being changed by the ready availability of fast foods, the relative cheapness of meat and high fat content food, and inadequate time for food preparation. This results in a high intake of "empty calories", which, together with reduced physical activity, is manifesting in the growing prevalence of non-communicable diseases like obesity, hypertension, and diabetes.[40]

A small proportion of respondents in all three locations indicated that they normally obtained food from shared meals and social networks. Borrowing food played a very minor role in all locations, although it seemed to be slightly more prevalent in the Inner City. Sharing among neighbours was slightly more prevalent in Alexandra than in Orange Farm and the Inner City. Both of these categories reflect the value of social capital in leveraging access to resources including food. Households in Alexandra were more likely to have obtained food through social networks than those in either Orange Farm or Inner City households, suggesting a stronger community network and greater social capital.

Community food kitchens were not visited frequently in any of the locations, although respondents in Alexandra indicated more frequent use than respondents from the other locations. This may reflect the lack of accessible community food kitchens in these areas. Among those who borrowed food or accessed it through community food kitchens, the majority indicated that this occurred quite frequently, at least once a month or more often.

This study's findings suggest that urban agriculture plays a very minor role as a source of food in the city. This may relate to difficulties accessing land and an unfavourable climate with low rainfall concentrated in 4 months of the year, followed by long, cold and dry winters. This is compounded by lack of relevant skills, ineffective agricultural extension services, lack of

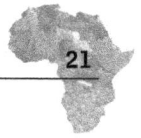

suitable financing for small-scale farming, and the risk of crop and equip-ment losses due to theft and vandalism. Urban agriculture as a source of food was most strongly present in Orange Farm, where 16% of house-holds reported that they grow some of their own food. Growing food was less prevalent in Alexandra, and almost totally absent in the Inner City. Orange Farm, located at the urban periphery, has far greater access to open spaces suitable for urban agriculture, which provided small-scale farmers with the opportunity to explore this option, whereas similar spaces in Alexandra are limited and marginal at best, and almost non-existent in the Inner City.[41]

7. FOOD INSECURITY AND HEALTH

Overall, 16% of households reported that a household member had been ill in the previous year. Morbidity levels were highest in the Inner City (17%) and lowest in Alexandra (15%). In identifying an illness, respon-dents were given four response categories (chronic, infectious, mental/physical disability and other). A large number of respondents identified the cause as "other" (76 of 181), suggesting either that there was a great deal of uncertainty about the 'actual' illness involved or that there had been no diagnosis. This, in turn, probably reflects poor access to health services to diagnose and treat illness. But the high percentage of "other" answers may also be because people were uncomfortable disclosing infor-mation due to the stigma attached to diseases such as HIV and AIDS.[42] Between 9-12% of the ill household members were household heads, with Alexandra and Orange Farm being more severely affected than the Inner City. In light of the small number of livelihood strategies typically engaged in by households, it is of concern that the most economically active group of people is most strongly affected by illness.

Mortality in the previous year was obviously lower than morbidity but was still significant (affecting 9% of surveyed households overall) (Figure 11). Orange Farm had clearly experienced the greatest number of deaths (in 12% of households), almost double the figure in the Inner City. Although not all of these deaths can be attributed to AIDS, there is a high preva-lence of infectious diseases such as TB and HIV and AIDS in the study areas. This reflects the rising tide of this double scourge in South African cities, with HIV prevalence in Gauteng at approximately 10.8% in 2005. Nationally, persons aged 15-49 years living in informal settlements have the highest HIV prevalence – 26% in 2005.[43] The 2008 national estimate of HIV prevalence among South Africans of all age groups is 10.6%. HIV prevalence peaked in females aged 25-29 years at 32.7% and for males it peaked at 25.8% in the 30-34-year-old age group. Gauteng has a prevalence of 10.3% among respondents over age 2.[44]

FIGURE 11: Household Burden of Morbidity and Mortality

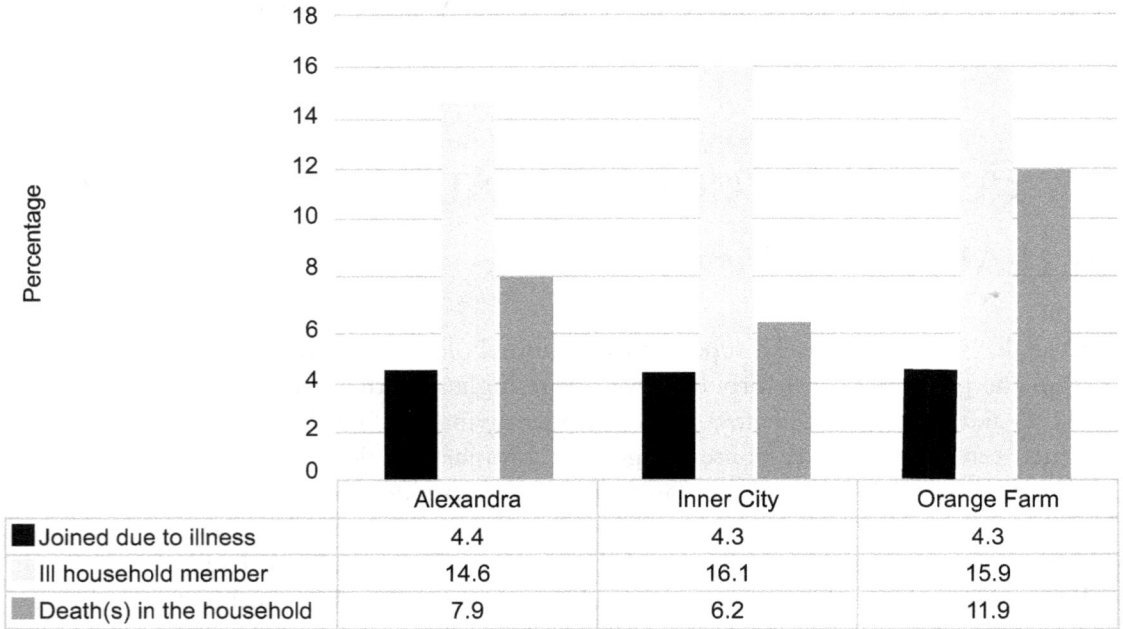

	Alexandra	Inner City	Orange Farm
Joined due to illness	4.4	4.3	4.3
Ill household member	14.6	16.1	15.9
Death(s) in the household	7.9	6.2	11.9

The other main health problem that emerged was a high prevalence of so-called "diseases of lifestyle" including diabetes, hypertension, heart disease, and arthritis. These patterns correspond with what has been characterised by Popkin as Stage 2 of the dietary transition.[45] These non-communicable diseases of lifestyle have also been related to transformations in food systems brought about by increased urbanisation and globalisation, including the growing consumption of highly-processed, calorie-dense starchy and fatty foods, preferences for fast foods and street foods shaped by commuting habits and time constraints, as well as changing patterns of physical activity related to more sedentary livelihoods and motorised transport systems.[46] The survey therefore confirmed the findings of other studies in South Africa that the city is experiencing a nutrition transition and that the resultant health problems are not diseases of affluence or lifestyle but diseases of poverty (unless poverty is considered a 'lifestyle').[47] The strong presence of asthma may reflect poor air quality, which is a combination of indoor air pollution due to paraffin and charcoal stoves, and environmental air pollution related to industry, vehicle exhaust fumes, dust, and chimney-smoke.

The illness or death of one or more household members can have a devastating impact on poor households. Statistical analysis of the Johannesburg data suggests that illness is correlated with food insecurity, although the causal connections can work in both directions. Households in the study who reported cases of infectious disease; mental illness, physical disability, or accidents; and 'other' illnesses were all more likely to be food insecure (Figure 12). Chronic diseases correlated much less strongly with food security status.

FIGURE 12: Food Security by Disease Status

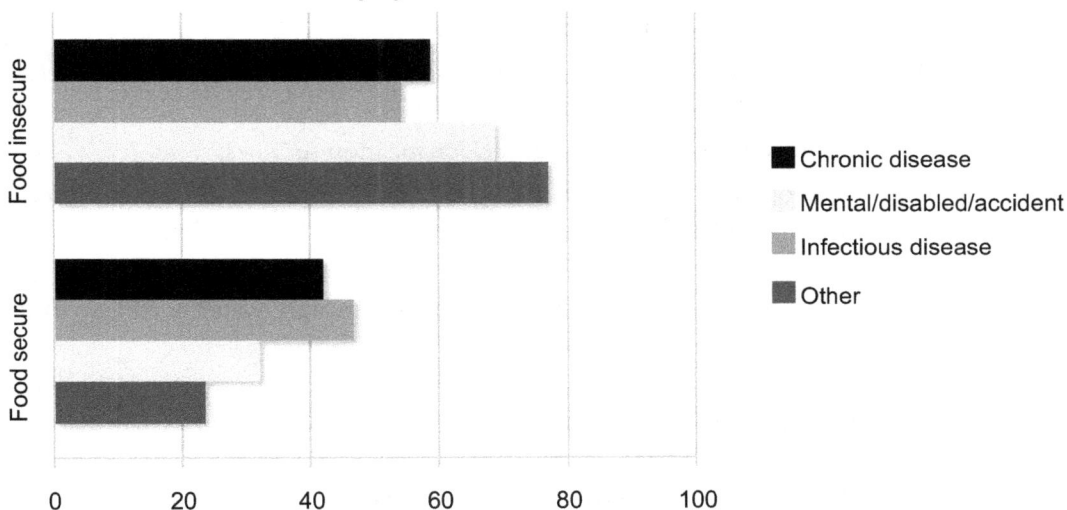

8. CONCLUSION

The levels of poverty and food insecurity in Johannesburg are unacceptably high and appear to be closely related to one another. A large proportion of the food insecure population is also highly vulnerable to shocks resulting from macro-economic trends (e.g. fuel price hikes), environmental change and health issues like HIV and AIDS, TB and chronic illness. Each of the three study areas had specific distinguishing characteristics. Some were related to the demographic profile of the population, but they were also likely to be a function of spatial and infrastructural factors. Strategies and policies to address food security and poverty should be informed by an appreciation of the complexity of the issues involved, and should address the specific features evident for each area.

The UJ urban livelihoods study reached several policy-related conclusions about food security in the city which are confirmed by this study. The UJ study identified the need for citywide policies that take a comprehensive approach to social development; recognised the importance of gathering intra-city or local-level data to inform community and ward-level planning and action; and called for more research and ongoing monitoring in the city-region. A recent review of food security policies and programmes in Gauteng argues for a greater degree of interdepartmental and intersectoral collaboration and communication to promote a more integrated and effective approach to implementing these recommendations.[48] This is also important to address the specific factors related to food security including:

Improve Infrastructure and Urban Form

- Improved local transport networks;
- Redesign settlements to a human-scale urban form that does not rely on access to private motorised transport;
- Enhance water, sanitation and electrification services;
- Develop central, secure and hygienic facilities for local fresh produce markets and informal food vendors, especially at commuter transit points;
- Integrate sustainable urban organic waste and water management with urban food production;
- Allocate space/land for urban gardens and informal markets in town planning and in architectural designs.

Enhance Economic Participation

- Implement measures to reduce or prevent sudden food price increases;
- Improve skills development;
- Enhance job placement and Expanded Public Works Programme linkages;
- Support the development of multiple livelihood strategies;
- Protect consumers from price-fixing, corporate collusion and speculation.

Enhance Communication, Social Capital and Social Mobilisation

- Encourage interdepartmental government collaborations;
- Employ appropriate and powerful media to improve public awareness and enhance mobilisation;
- Collectivise and socialise (e.g. in community food kitchens,

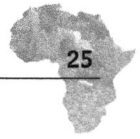

community gardens) the production, procurement, processing and consumption of healthy foods to develop greater social capital.

Improve Food Availability and Accessibility

- Enhance urban food production/urban agriculture training and research centres;
- Support the development of more resource-efficient, sustainable and resilient agricultural practices;
- Enhance and support the informal economy;
- Create linkages between local producers and markets;
- Develop food aid programmes and community kitchens accessible to the most vulnerable (elderly, grant recipients) as well as the wider community;
- Engage in public-relations campaigns that inform people about opportunities and procedures for accessing social services and food aid;
- Encourage the formation of food cooperatives and mutual aid strategies like *stokvels*.

Improve Food Utilisation

- Enhance the public image of healthy food culture with a focus on diversity including whole grains, tubers, pulses, fresh fruit and vegetables;
- Develop more effective nutritional education programmes integrated with the empowerment of informal vendors, community food kitchens and feeding schemes;
- Develop health promotion programmes that protect the economically active population;
- Provide households affected by infectious illnesses, mental illness and physical disability with additional support, e.g. food packages, food coupons, job training and placement;
- Regulate fast-food chains and consumer food brands to adhere to healthy and ethical nutritional business practices;
- Research into understanding and monitoring food security;
- Training to develop social and institutional capacity to address food utilisation issues.

In conclusion, while the state has a constitutional mandate (Chapter 2, Section 27.1b) to ensure that all citizens are food secure, it is only through a broad participatory approach that pro-actively engages all levels of society that the ecological, social and financial resources to implement these recommendations can be mobilised. Food insecurity concerns all residents of South Africa. All South Africans, and the population of Johannesburg in particular, are in a position of great social strain. Recent xenophobic violence and strikes about poor services, and the political turmoil in North Africa in 2011 provide a glimpse of the social upheavals that could occur if the issues of urban poverty, economic participation, and food security are not addressed timeously and effectively.

ENDNOTES

1   See http://www.joburg.org.za

2   Gauteng Provincial Government, *A Growth and Development Strategy (GDS) for the Gauteng Province* (Johannesburg: Gauteng Provincial Government, 2005).

3   T. De Wet, L. Patel, M. Korth and C. Forrester, *Johannesburg Poverty and Livelihoods Study* (Johannesburg: Centre for Social Development in Africa, 2008).

4   T. Brinkhoff, "The Principal Agglomerations of the World" at http://www.citypopulation.de/world/Agglomerations.html; J. Beaverstock, R. Smith and P. Taylor, "A Roster of World Cities" *Cities* 16(6) (1999): 445-58.

5   Government Communication and Information System (GCIS), "2010 Communication Project Management Unit" at http://www.sa2010.gov.za/southafrica/hostcities.php

6   City of Johannesburg, *Human Development Strategy: Joburg's Commitment to the Poor Office of the City Manager* (Johannesburg: City of Johannesburg, 2005).

7   Statistics SA, "Community Survey, 2007. Basic Results: Municipalities," Pretoria, 2008.

8   See J. Beall, O. Crankshaw and S. Parnell, "The Causes of Unemployment in Post Apartheid Johannesburg and the Livelihood Strategies of the Poor" *Tijdschrift voor Economiche en Sociale Geografie* 91(4) (2000): 379-96; P. Bond, "Johannesburg: Of Gold and Gangsters" In M. Davis and D. Monk, eds., *Evil Paradises: The Dreamworlds of Neoliberalism* (New York: New Press, 2007), pp1-23; M. Murray, "Fire and Ice: Unnatural Disasters and the Disposable Urban Poor in Post-Apartheid Johannesburg" *International Journal of Urban and Regional Research* 33(1) (2009): 165-92.

9   K. Beavon, *Johannesburg: The Making and Shaping of the City* (Pretoria: University of South Africa Press, 2004).

10 J. Beall, O. Crankshaw and S. Parnell, "Local Government, Poverty Reduction and Inequality in Johannesburg" *Environment and Urbanization* 12(1) (2000): 107-22; B. Lipeitz, "Building a Vision for the Post?Apartheid City: What Role for Participation in Johannesburg's City Development Strategy?" *International Journal of Urban and Regional Research* 32(1) (2008): 135–63; M. Murray, *City of Extremes: The Spatial Politics of Johannesburg* (Johannesburg: Wits University Press, 2011).

11 De Wet et al, *Johannesburg Poverty and Livelihoods Study*, p.4.

12 Centre on Housing Rights and Evictions, "Any Room for the Poor? Forced Evictions in Johannesburg, South Africa" Johannesburg, 2005, p.19.

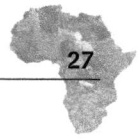

13   S. Parnell, "Building Developmental Local Government to Fight Poverty: Institutional Change in the City of Johannesburg" *International Development Planning Review* 26(4) (2004): 377-99; S. Parnell and J. Robinson, "Development and Urban Policy: Johannesburg's City Development Strategy" *Urban Studies* 43 (2006): 337-56.

14   City of Johannesburg, "Human Development Strategy: Joburg's Commitment to the Poor" Office of the City Manager, Johannesburg, 2005, p. 26f.

15   S. Greenberg, "Urban Food Politics, Welfare and Resistance: A Case Study of the Southern Johannesburg Metro" Grant Report, Centre for Civil Society, University of Kwazulu Natal, 2006.

16   J. Crush and B. Frayne, *The Invisible Crisis: Urban Food Security in Southern Africa*, AFSUN Series No. 1, Cape Town, 2010.

17   Speech by the Executive Mayor, Cllr Amos Masondo, on the occasion of the inner city summit, Braamfontein Recreation Centre, Johannesburg, 5 May 2007, at http://www.joburg.org.za/index.php?option=com_content&task=view&id=756&Itemid=9

18   De Wet et al, *Johannesburg Poverty and Livelihood Study*.

19   P. Bonner and N. Nieftagodien, *Alexandra: A History* (Johannesburg: Wits University Press, 2009).

20   M. Roefs, V. Naidoo, M. Meyer and J. Makalela, "Alexandra: A Case Study of Urban Renewal for the Presidential 10 Year Review Project" 2003, p. 19.

21   P. Morris, "Alexandra Township – A History, Lessons for Urban Renewal and Some Challenges for Planners" Paper presented at Planning for Reconstruction and Transformation Conference, Durban, 2000.

22   C. Onyango, "Urban and Peri-urban Agriculture as a Poverty Alleviation Strategy among Low Income Households: The Case of Orange Farm, South Johannesburg" Unpublished PhD Thesis, University of South Africa, Cape Town, 2010, p.78f.

23   B. Frayne et al, *The State of Food Insecurity in Southern African Cities* (Cape Town: AFSUN, 2010).

24   In 2007, 1.5% of South African households were headed by children between 12 and 18; see S. Mogotlane, M. Chauke, G. van Rensburg, S. Human and C. Kganakga, "A Situational Analysis of Child-Headed Households in South Africa" *Curations* 33(3) (2010): 24-32.

25   M. Murray, *Taming the Disorderly City: The Spatial Landscape of Johannesburg after Apartheid* (Ithaca: Cornell University Press, 2008), p. 107.

26   J. Coates, A. Swindale and P. Bilinsky, "Household Food Insecurity Access Scale (HFIAS) for Measurement of Food Access: Indicator Guide (Version 3)" Food and Nutrition Technical Assistance Project (FANTA), Academy for Educational Development, Washington, DC, 2007, p.18.

27   De Wet et al., *Johannesburg Poverty and Livelihoods Study,* pp. 6-7.

28   Ibid, pp.6-7.

29   Afrobarometer, "Lived Poverty in Africa: Desperation, Hope and Patience" Briefing Paper No. 11, University of Cape Town, Cape Town, 2004.

30   A. Swindale and P. Bilinsky, "Household Dietary Diversity Score (HDDS) for Measurement of Household Food Access: Indicator Guide (Version 2)" Food

and Nutrition Technical Assistance Project (FANTA), Academy for Educational Development, Washington, DC, 2006.

31   N. Steyn, J. Nel, G. Nantel, G. Kennedy and D. Labadarios, "Food Variety and Dietary Diversity Scores in Children: Are they Good Indicators of Dietary Adequacy? *Public Health Nutrition* 9(5): 644-50.

32   P. Bilinsky and A. Swindale, "Months of Adequate Household Food Provisioning (MAHFP) for Measurement of Household Food Access: Indicator Guide" Food and Nutrition Technical Assistance Project (FANTA), Academy for Educational Development, Washington, DC, 2007.

33   Statistics SA, "Income and Expenditure of Households 2005/2006" Statistical Release P0100, Pretoria, 2008.

34   M. Chopra, "Globalization, Urbanization and Nutritional Change South Africa Case Study" In FAO, *Globalisation of Food Systems in Developing Countries: Impact on Food Security and Nutrition* (Rome: FAO, 2004), p121.

35   C. van Rooyen and B. Mavhandu, "The Informal Food Marketing System in Urban Environments: Case Studies of Kagiso and Orange Farm" *Development Southern Africa* 14(3) (1997): 471-6; J. Crush and B. Frayne, *Pathways to Insecurity: Urban Food Supply and Access in Southern African Cities,* AFSUN Series No. 3, Cape Town, 2010.

36   Crush and Frayne, *Pathways to Insecurity.*

37   M. Ruel and J. Garrett, "Features of Urban Food and Nutrition Security and Considerations for Successful Urban Programming" In FAO, *Globalisation of Food Systems in Developing Countries: Impact on Food Security and Nutrition* (Rome: FAO, 2004), p. 39.

38   FAO, *Globalisation of Food Systems in Developing Countries*, p. 18.

39   D. Labadarios, ed., *The National Food Consumption Survey (NFCS): Children Aged 1-9 Years South Africa, 1999* (Stellenbosch: NFCS, Department of Health, 2000).

40   Chopra, "Globalization, Urbanization and Nutritional Change."

41   Onyango, "Urban and Peri-urban Agriculture as a Poverty Alleviation Strategy among Low Income Households: The Case of Orange Farm, South Johannesburg."

42   See C. Varga, G. Sherman and S. Jones, "HIV-Disclosure in the Context of Vertical Transmission: HIV-Positive Mothers in Johannesburg, South Africa" *AIDS Care* 18(8) (2006): 952-60; A. Mahajan, J. Sayles, V. Patel, R. Remien, D. Ortiz, G. Szekeres and T. Coates, "Stigma in the HIV/AIDS Epidemic: A Review of the Literature and Recommendations for the Way Forward" *AIDS* 22(Suppl 2) (2008): S67-S79.

43   P. Banati, "Risk Amplification: HIV in Migrant Communities" *Development Southern Africa* 24(1) (2007): 205-23; Human Sciences Research Council, "South African National HIV Prevalence, HIV Incidence, Behaviour and Communication Survey, 2005" Cape Town, 2005, p35.

44   HSRC, "South African National HIV Prevalence, Incidence, Behaviour and Communication Survey, 2008: A Turning Tide among Teenagers?" Cape Town, 2008, p48.

45   B. Popkin, "The Nutrition Transition in the Developing World" *Development Policy Review* 21(5/6) (2003): 581-97.

46   G. Kennedy, G. Nantel and P. Shetty, "Globalization of Food Systems

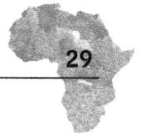

in Developing Countries: A Synthesis of Country Case Studies" In FAO, *Globalisation of Food Systems in Developing Countries: Impact on Food Security and Nutrition* (Rome: FAO, 2004); P. Amuna and F. Zotor, "Epidemiological and Nutrition Transition Developing Countries: Impact on Human Health and Development" *Proceedings of the Nutrition Society* 67 (2008): 82–90; A. Aikins, N. Unwin, C. Agyeman, P. Allotey, C. Campbell and D. Arhinful, "Tackling Africa's Chronic Disease Burden: From the Local to the Global" *Globalization and Health* 6(5) (2010): 1-7; I. Tewfik, A. Bener and S. Tewfik, "Is Africa Facing a Nutrition Transition under the Double Burden of Disease?" In A. Ahmed and S. Nwankwo, eds., *Achieving Sustainable Development in Africa* (London: World Association for Sustainable Development, 2010), pp. 160-171; J. Crush, B. Frayne and M. McLachlan, *Rapid Urbanization and the Nutrition Transition in Southern Africa*. AFSUN Series No. 7, Cape Town, 2011.

47   L. Bourne, E. Lambert and K. Steyn, "Where Does the Black Population of South Africa Stand on the Nutrition Transition?" *Public Health Nutrition* 5 (2002): 157-62; K. Steyn, J. Fourie and N. Temple, eds., *Chronic Diseases of Lifestyle in South Africa: 1995 - 2005* (Cape Town: South African Medical Research Council, 2006), pp. 33-47.

48   Siyakhana Initiative, "Gauteng Food Security Policy Review" Unpublished Paper, Gauteng City Region Observatory for the Gauteng Department of Economic Development, 2011.

www.ingramcontent.com/pod-product-compliance
Lightning Source LLC
Chambersburg PA
CBHW080135270326
41926CB00021B/4498